Friends and Mates in Fifty States

Ellen Weisberg

2009

Ken Yoffe

Galde Press, Inc.
PO Box 460
Lakeville, Minnesota 55044–0460
www.galdepress.com

Introduction

Welcome to the United States of America (U.S.A.)! The U.S.A. is the third largest country in the world, and one of the most beautiful. It is full of lakes and rivers, mountains and canyons, beaches and deserts. It has many different trees and flowers, and all sorts of different crops we use as food. And, of course, America has birds and animals of all kinds. Last, but not least, the United States has about 300 million people, from many different backgrounds and cultures.

In this book, you'll meet five adventurous friends: Wandering Willy, Nosy Normie, Meandering Mickey, Sightseeing Susie, and Exploring Ellie. They will help you learn about the land, cities, animals, and other wonderful things in each of the fifty states in the U.S.A. Along the way, you'll also meet other friends of theirs, each of whom will host Willy, Normie, Mickey, Susie, or Ellie and teach them (and you) about his or her home state. These fifty friends of theirs are very special, because they are each named after the capital city of their state!

Enjoy the trip!

Acknowledgements

With love, to
our daughter, Emily,

Emily's loving grandparents, Nana Sheila, Poppy Joe, Nana Susan, Grandpa Dan, Safta Karen and Saba Harvey, and Emily's loving aunties and uncles, Jane, Jeff, Jonathan, Larry, Rachel, and Sarah.

In addition, we wish to thank Suzanne and Alex Meyer, Dorna Baumann, Mike and Stacey Smalley, Rob Carolan, John Soldner, Kristen Kerouac, Allison Anneser, Cindy Brunelle, Jennifer Metcalf, Jane Nikander, Leona Palmer, Mary Small, Laurie Toupin, Jiangru Jiang, and Lizi and Jenny (Little Miss Des Moines) Wu for their inspiration and valuable feedback for *Friends and Mates in Fifty States*.

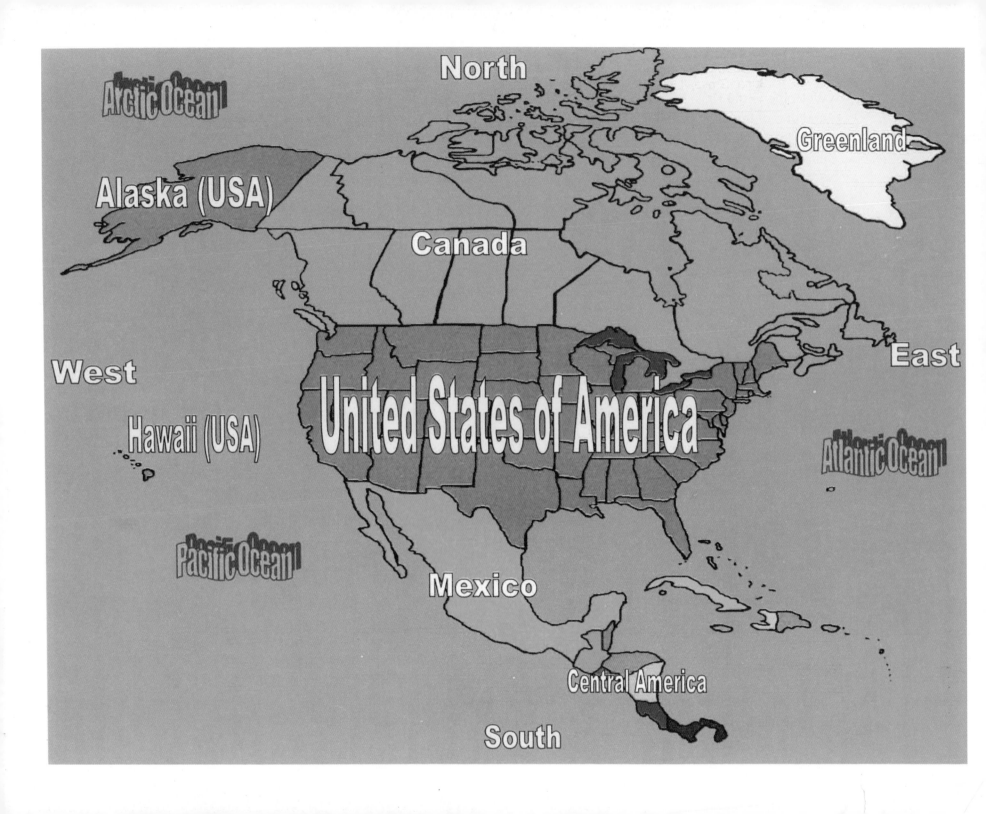

Willie

Susie

Normie

Mickey

**Exploring Ellie and Wandering Willie
travel to places both warm and chilly.
For Normie and Susie there's water and sand
While meandering Mickey tours the heartland.
The five boys and girls visit friends and mates
named after the capital of each of the states.**

Ellie

Wandering Through the West with Willie

Willie will serve as guide and host
from the Rocky Mountains to the Western Coast.
In Hawaii and Alaska he'll take a quick rest,
and then he's off to the Pacific Northwest.

Willie

CANADA

Northwest

Rockies

Pacific Ocean

West Coast

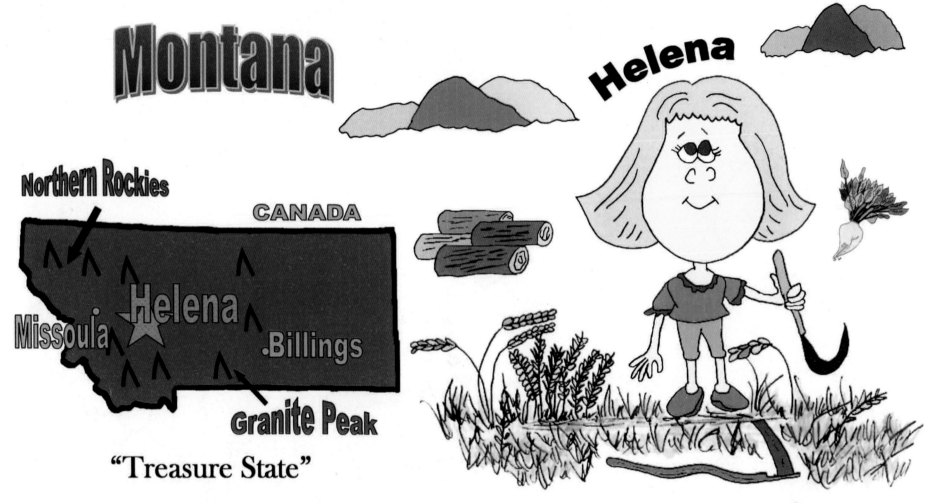

Montana

Northern Rockies

CANADA

Missoula ★ **Helena** .Billings

Granite Peak

"Treasure State"

Helena

Helena grew sugar beets, barley, and wheat
just east of the Rockies and near Granite Peak.
Her family in Billings sold lumber and wood.
Life in Montana was wholesome and good.

cattle

Montana

Forty-first State

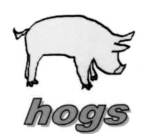

hogs

Bird: Western Meadowlark

Tree: Ponderosa Pine

Flower: Bitterroot

mining

oil

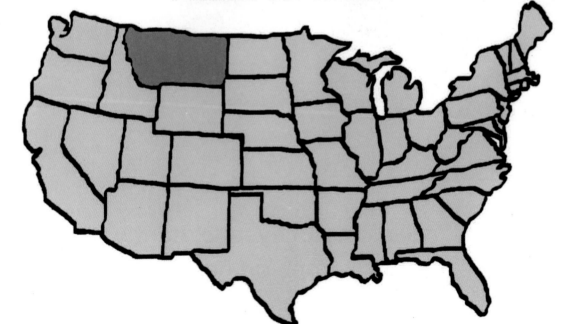

Wyoming

Yellowstone National Park

Sheridan

Rockies

Casper

Laramie

★ Cheyenne

Cheyenne

"Equality State"

Shy, shy Cheyenne, hardly making a peep,
grows crops on her farm, with her cattle and sheep.
She walks past cottonwoods and a loud meadowlark,
and crosses the mountains to Yellowstone Park.

 mining

Wyoming

Forty-Fourth State

 lumber

wheat

Bird: Western Meadowlark
Tree: Cottonwood
Flower: Indian Paintbrush

oil

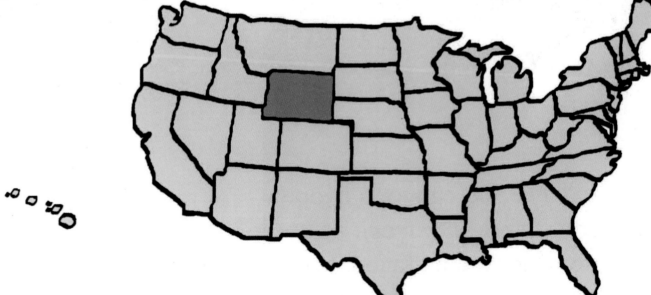

Colorado

"Colorful Colorado"
"Centennial State"

Denver hikes through valleys and canyons deep.
He climbs the Rocky Mountains, with faces so steep.
Through Boulder and Fort Collins, he takes it slow.
He continues to Mount Elbert, and then Pueblo.

Colorado

Thirty-eighth State

gold

cattle

corn

Bird: Lark Bunting
Tree: Blue Spruce
Flower: Rocky Mountain Columbine

wheat

New Mexico

Santa Fe

Albuquerque°

Las Cruces

MEXICO

"Land of Enchantment"

Santa Fe was angry mainly because
his neighbors kept calling him Santa Claus.
Fetching his chilies, with movements quite jerky,
he fled from Las Cruces to Albuquerque.

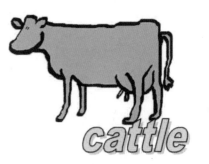

New Mexico

cattle

Bird: Roadrunner
Tree: Pinyon Pine
Flower: Yucca Flower

COAL

oil

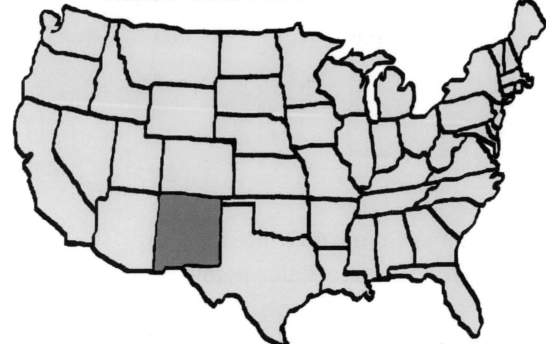

Phoenix likes to go to the Colorado Plateau
to see the Grand Canyon and the River below.
Yuma, Arizona, is nice to pass through.
Tucson and Flagstaff are quite pleasant, too.

Arizona

Forty-Eighth State

Bird: Cactus Wren

Tree: Yellow Palo Verde

Flower: Saguaro Cactus Blossom

cotton

cattle

mining

Miss Salt Lake would just cry and cry
the biggest of tears that never would dry.
Into the Lake the tears did flow,
not far from King's Peak and the Wasatch Plateau.

Utah

Forty-fifth State

Bird: Sea Gull
Tree: Blue Spruce
Flower: Sego Lily

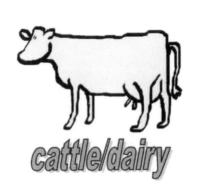
cattle/dairy

turkeys

oil

mining

Carson traveled wide in search of a casino.

He went down to Las Vegas from his hometown up in Reno.

He had a lot of fun with the dice he'd shake and throw.

Then he wandered back up north to greater Lake Tahoe.

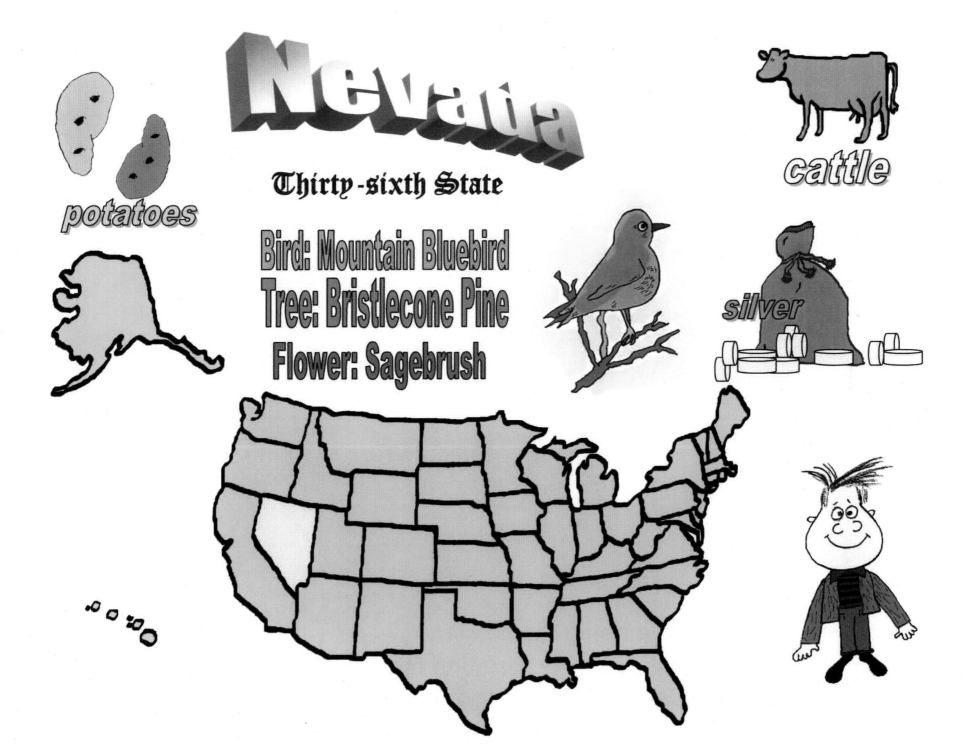

Nevada

Thirty-sixth State

Bird: Mountain Bluebird
Tree: Bristlecone Pine
Flower: Sagebrush

potatoes

cattle

silver

California

Sacramento

Redding

Sacramento

San Francisco Bay →

San Jose

Pacific Ocean

Bakersfield

Los Angeles/Hollywood

"Golden State"

San Diego

Mexico

Sacramento is so grand, a rising movie star.
Her beauty and ability have gotten her quite far.
All her fans in Bakersfield, as well as San Jose
follow her from Hollywood to San Francisco Bay.

California

Thirty-first State

grapes

cattle

Bird: California Valley Quail
Tree: Redwood
Flower: California Poppy

oil

Honolulu munches on a macadamia nut,
sitting in the middle of a quiet, thatch-roofed hut.
She climbs up Mauna Kea and stares into its crater,
and holds a piece of sugar cane she plans to each much later.

glass, clay, stone products

Hawaii

Fiftieth State

Bird: Nene

Tree: Candlenut Tree

Flower: Hibiscus

pineapple

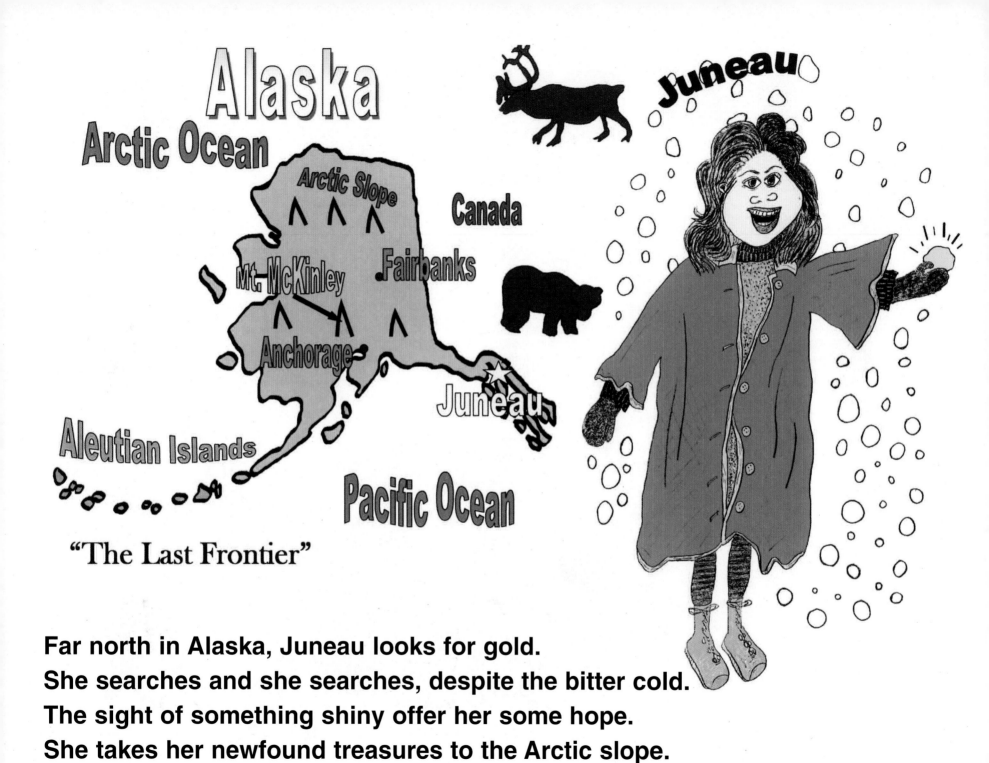

Far north in Alaska, Juneau looks for gold.
She searches and she searches, despite the bitter cold.
The sight of something shiny offer her some hope.
She takes her newfound treasures to the Arctic slope.

Alaska

seafood

lumber

Forty-ninth State

Bird: Willow Ptarmigan

Tree: Sitka Spruce

Flower: Forget Me Not

oil

mining

Washington

CANADA

Puget Sound

Seattle

Spokane

Mt. Rainier

Olympia

Pacific Ocean

"Evergreen State"

Olympia watches rain drops
on the Puget Sound.
The drizzle in Seattle
seems to always hang around.
But Mt. Ranier in the distance
and Pacific Coast so near,
are why Olympia holds her
state of Washington so dear.

Mama Salem walks right near a tall volcanic peak
while her children run around, playing hide and seek.
To Oregon's Blue Mountains they all will make their way
and then they go to Crater Lake to finish up their day.

lumber

Oregon

cattle

Thirty-third State

Bird: Western Meadowlark
Tree: Douglas Fir
Flower: Oregon Grape

wheat

Boise lugs potatoes and many different grains
south of the mountains, to the Snake River Plains.
He passes a few canyons and gorges on the way
and rests in Twin Falls, Idaho, calling it a day.

barley

lumber

Idaho

Forty-third State

Bird: Mountain Bluebird

Tree: Western White Pine

Flower: Syringa

wheat

cattle

silver

beets

Nosing into the North with Normie

Normie has friends in the Northern Plains states and Wisconsin and Michigan, south of the Lakes. The Dakotas, Minnesota and Canada nearby will bring a joyous tear to young Normie's eye.

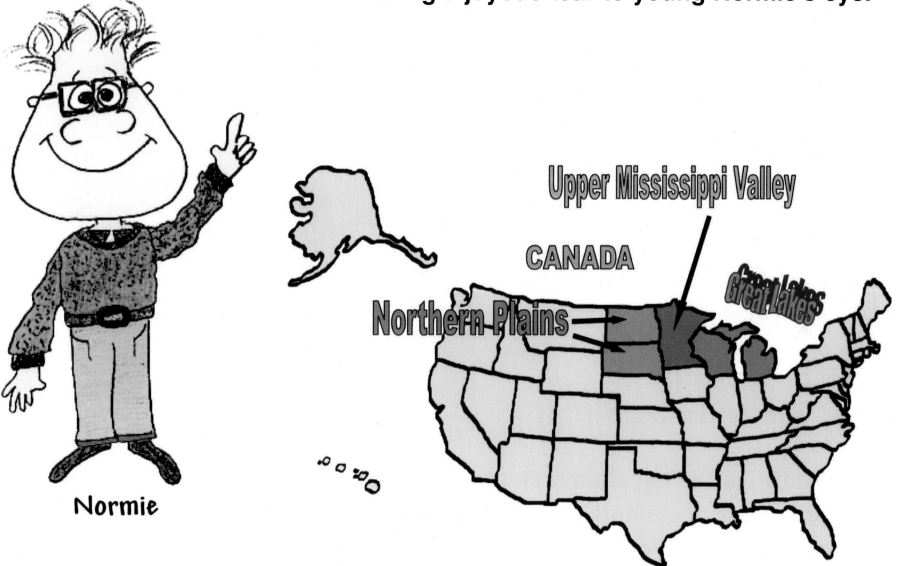

Normie

North Dakota

CANADA

Minot

Grand Forks

Badlands

Red River Valley

Bismarck

Fargo

Bismarck

"Flickertail State"

"Peace Garden State"

"Roughrider State"

In the Red River Valley, Bismarck grows his wheat.
There are sugar beets and barley, and lots of corn to eat.
In Fargo and Grand Forks he stays for quite a while,
before he tours the Badlands with his big, happy smile.

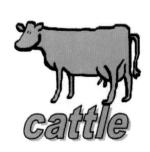
cattle

North Dakota

Thirty-ninth State

mining

Bird: Western Meadowlark
Tree: American Elm
Flower: Wild Prairie Rose

sunflowers

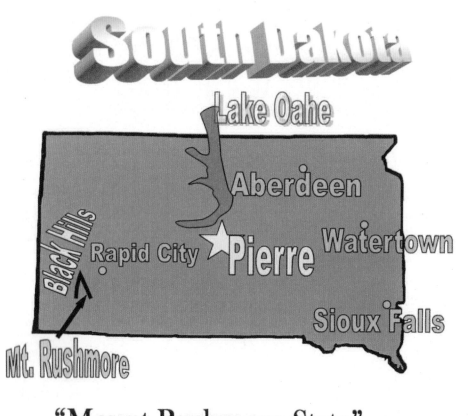

South Dakota

Lake Oahe

Aberdeen

Black Hills

Rapid City ★Pierre Watertown

Sioux Falls

Mt. Rushmore

"Mount Rushmore State"

Pierre wanders through the
Black Hills in the west.
Then he travels eastward,
continuing his quest.
Sioux Falls, Rapid City,
Watertown, and Aberdeen
are just a few of South Dakota's
places that he's seen.

Pierre

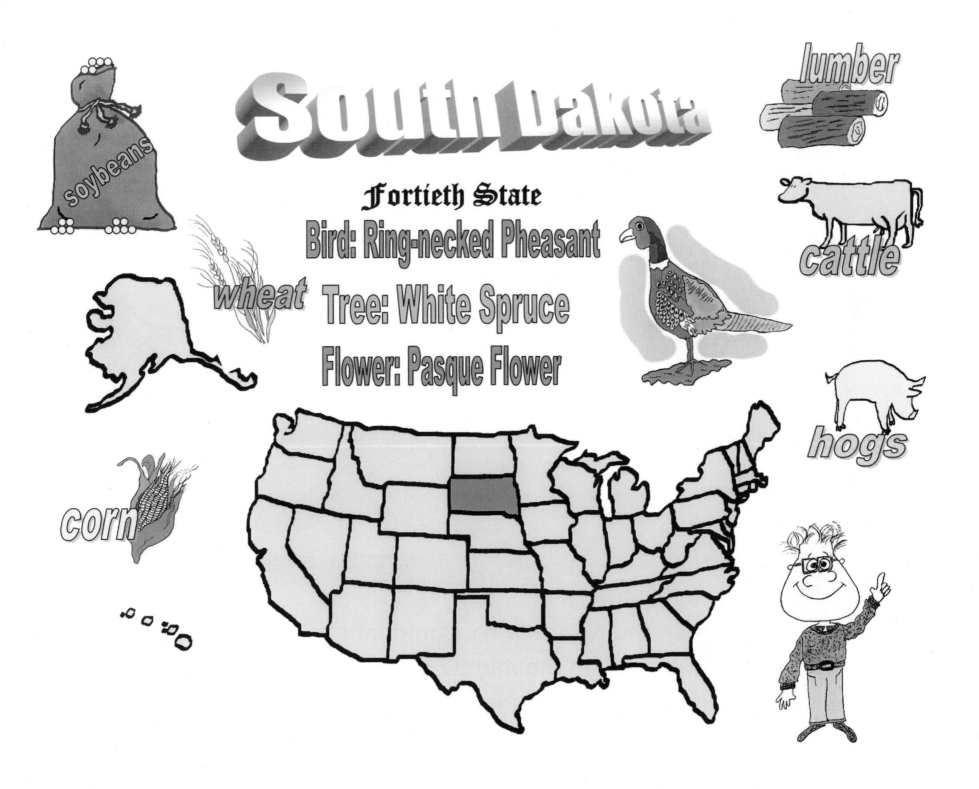

Minnie was Paul's sister, the twin that he would miff.
The two were always fighting, in the middle of a tiff.
Up on Eagle Mountain, he'd taunt her endlessly
and irk her from Duluth all the way to Albert Lea.

Minnesota

Thirty-second state

Bird: Common Loon

Tree: Red Pine

Flower: Pink and White Lady's-Slipper

cattle/dairy

turkeys

wheat

corn

hogs

soybeans

Madison, from Wisconsin, lives out near Green Bay.
She travels into Oshkosh day after day.
She takes some fancy cheese, and cranberries, and corn
up toward Lake Superior, where she had been born.

WisCOnsin

Thirtieth State

hogs

cattle

Bird: Robin
Tree: Sugar Maple
Flower: Wood Violet

paper products

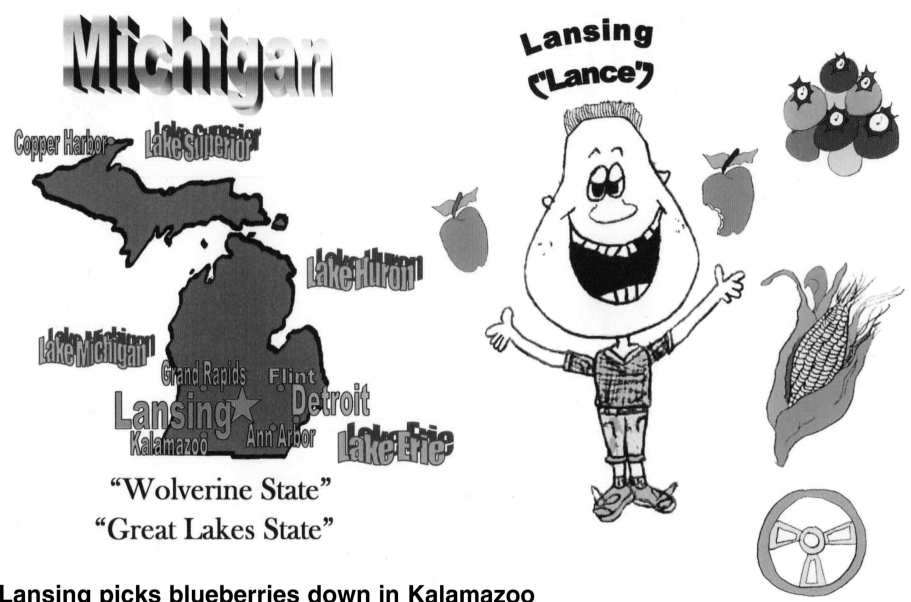

Lansing picks blueberries down in Kalamazoo
then apples in Flint, and Grand Rapids, too.
He buys cars in Detroit, husks corn in Ann Arbor,
and strolls by the waters right off from Copper Harbor.

Michigan

Twenty-sixth State

soybeans

cattle

Bird: Robin

Tree: Eastern White Pine

Flower: Apple Blossom

hogs

Meandering Through the Midwest with Mickey

In the Ohio Valley, Mickey starts his day.
Then toward the central plains he slowly makes his way.
He passes Illinois, Iowa, and Missouri.
Nebraska and Kansas will finish up his journey.

Mickey

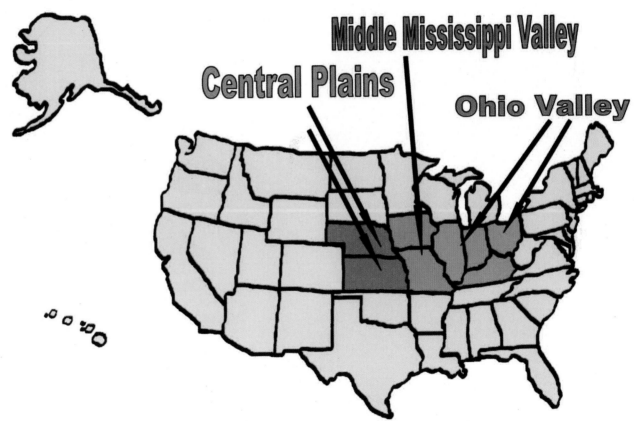

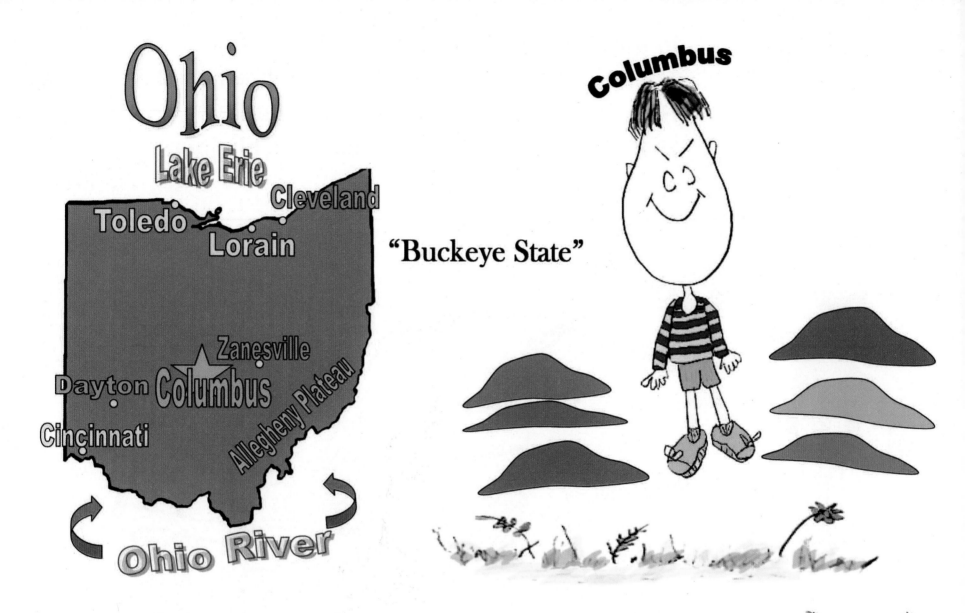

Ohio

Lake Erie

Cleveland

Toledo

Lorain

"Buckeye State"

Columbus

Zanesville

Dayton Columbus

Allegheny Plateau

Cincinnati

Ohio River

Columbus takes a walk on the green rolling plain,
past the town of Zanesville, and north toward Lorain.
He heads back down to Dayton, then up near Toledo.
Before he knows what's happening, he's seen all of Ohio.

 cattle/dairy

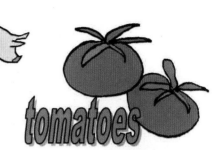 hogs

Ohio

tomatoes

eggs and poultry

Seventeenth State

Bird: Cardinal

Tree: Ohio Buckeye

Flower: Scarlet Carnation

 soybeans

corn

Frankfort ("Frank")

Kentucky

"Bluegrass State"

Frankfort lives in Lexington with horses in a barn.
He raises hogs and grows tall corn on a little farm.
When the pigs have all been fed and stables have been cleaned
he takes a break and heads out west to visit Bowling Green.

Kentucky

Fifteenth State

cattle

Bird: Cardinal
Tree: Yellow Poplar
Flower: Goldenrod

soybeans

tobacco

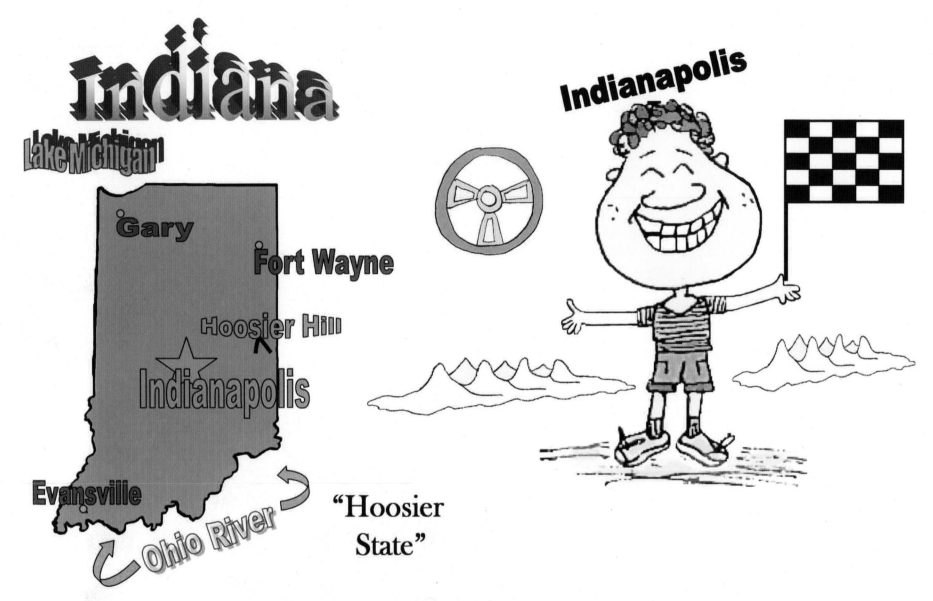

Indianapolis drove quite fast, and headed to Fort Wayne
while cruising past the northern dunes and central rolling plain.
He took in all the scenes when he stopped at Hoosier Hill.
He traveled up to Gary, and then down to Evansville.

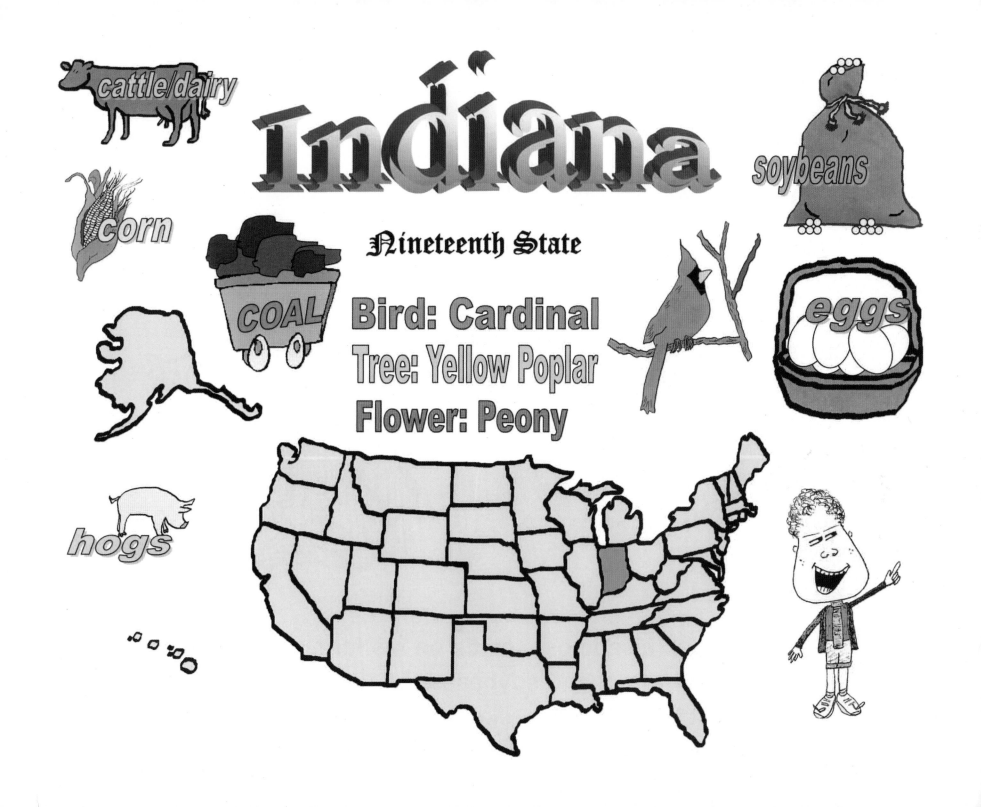

cattle/dairy

corn

Indiana

soybeans

COAL

Nineteenth State

eggs

Bird: Cardinal
Tree: Yellow Poplar
Flower: Peony

hogs

Illinois

Charles Mound

Chicago

Champaign

Springfield

Mississippi River

Ohio River

Springfield

Soybeans

"Prairie State"
"Land of Lincoln"

Springfield raised some cattle on his farm near by Charles Mound.
He planted wheat and soybeans, on very fertile ground.
He'd visit big, big cities, like Chicago and Champaign,
then walk on open hills, the prairies and the plains.

corn

Illinois

Twenty-first State

COAL

Bird: Cardinal
Tree: White Oak
Flower: Purple Violet

hogs

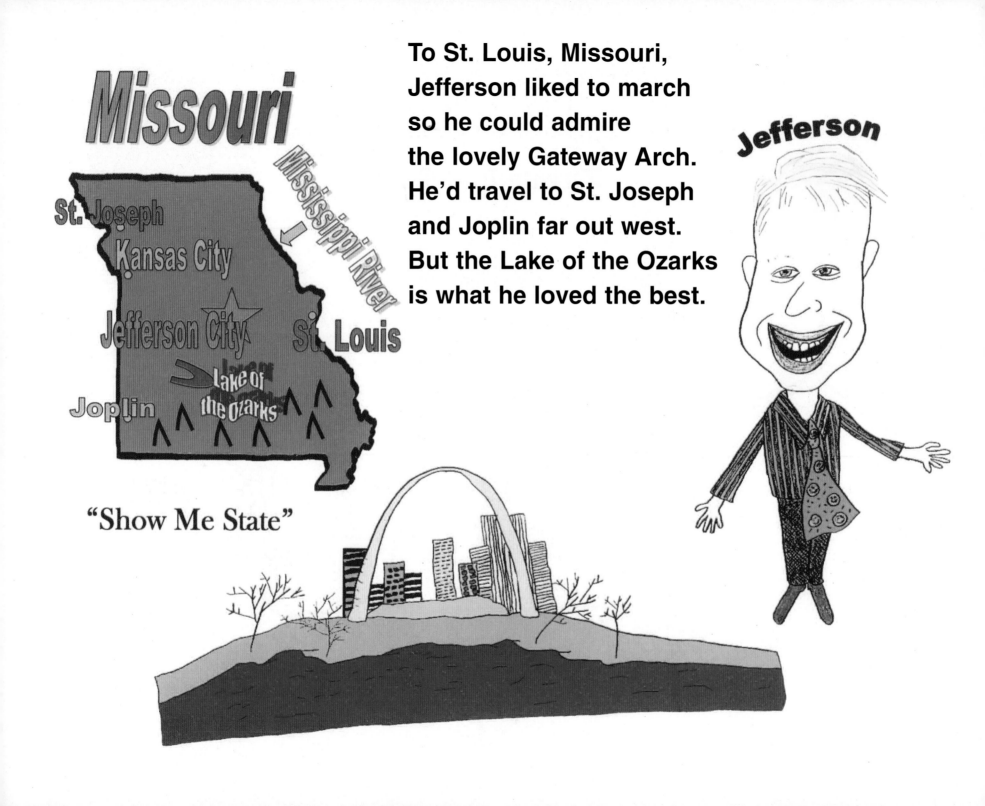

Missouri

Mississippi River

St. Joseph

Kansas City

Jefferson City

St. Louis

Joplin

Lake of the Ozarks

"Show Me State"

To St. Louis, Missouri,
Jefferson liked to march
so he could admire
the lovely Gateway Arch.
He'd travel to St. Joseph
and Joplin far out west.
But the Lake of the Ozarks
is what he loved the best.

Jefferson

Missouri

Twenty-fourth State

soybeans

cattle

corn

hogs

Bird: Bluebird

Tree: Flowering Dogwood

Flower: Hawthorn

eggs and poultry

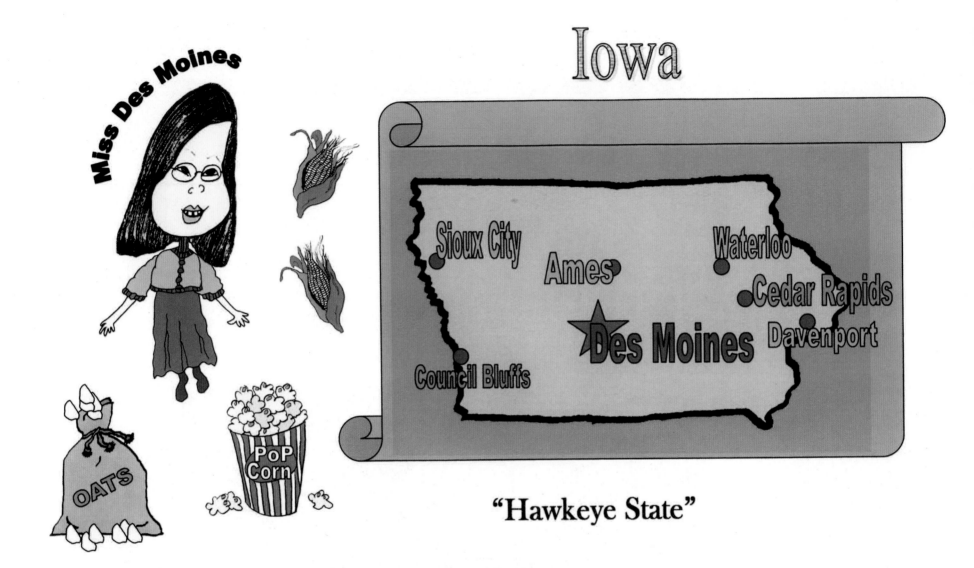

Iowa

Miss Des Moines

Sioux City · Ames · Waterloo · Cedar Rapids · Des Moines · Davenport · Council Bluffs

OATS

PoP Corn

"Hawkeye State"

Little Miss Des Moines finds quite a lot to do
in the towns of Davenport, Ames, and Waterloo.
She buys oats in Cedar Rapids, pops corn in Sioux City.
and the trip down to Council Bluffs makes her feel giddy.

cattle

Iowa

Twenty-ninth State

soybeans

Bird: Eastern Goldfinch
Tree: Oak
Flower: Wild Prairie Rose

hogs

Nebraska

Lincoln

"Cornhusker's State"

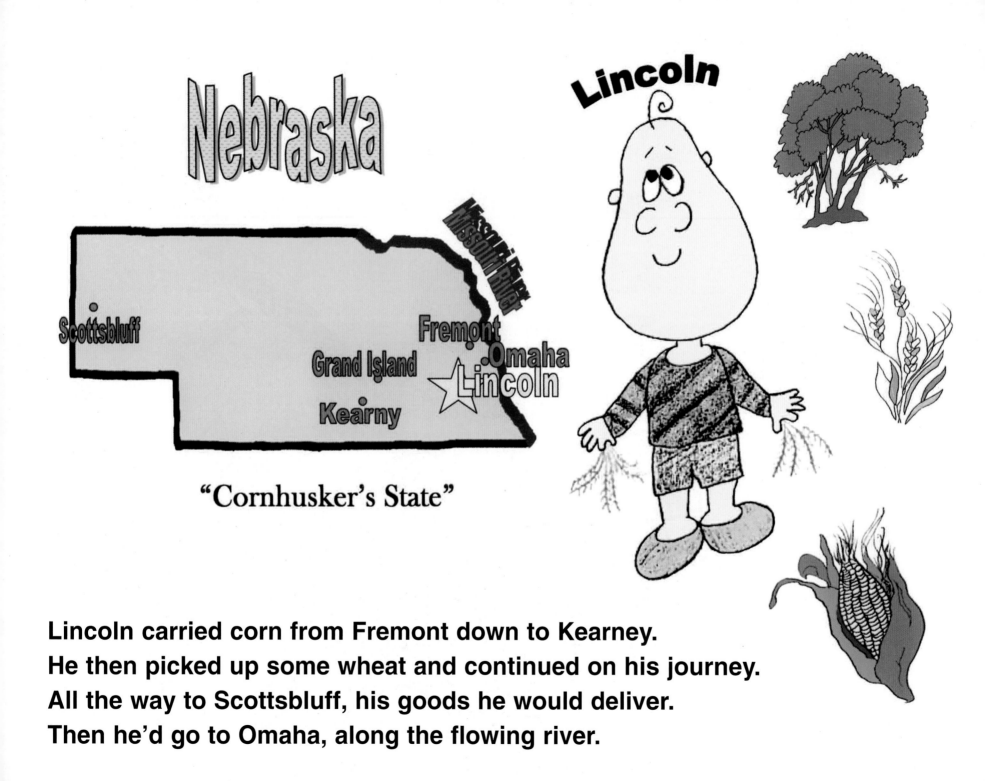

Lincoln carried corn from Fremont down to Kearney.
He then picked up some wheat and continued on his journey.
All the way to Scottsbluff, his goods he would deliver.
Then he'd go to Omaha, along the flowing river.

hogs

Nebraska

cattle

Thirty-seventh State

Bird: Western Meadowlark

Tree: Cottonwood

Flower: Goldenrod

soybeans

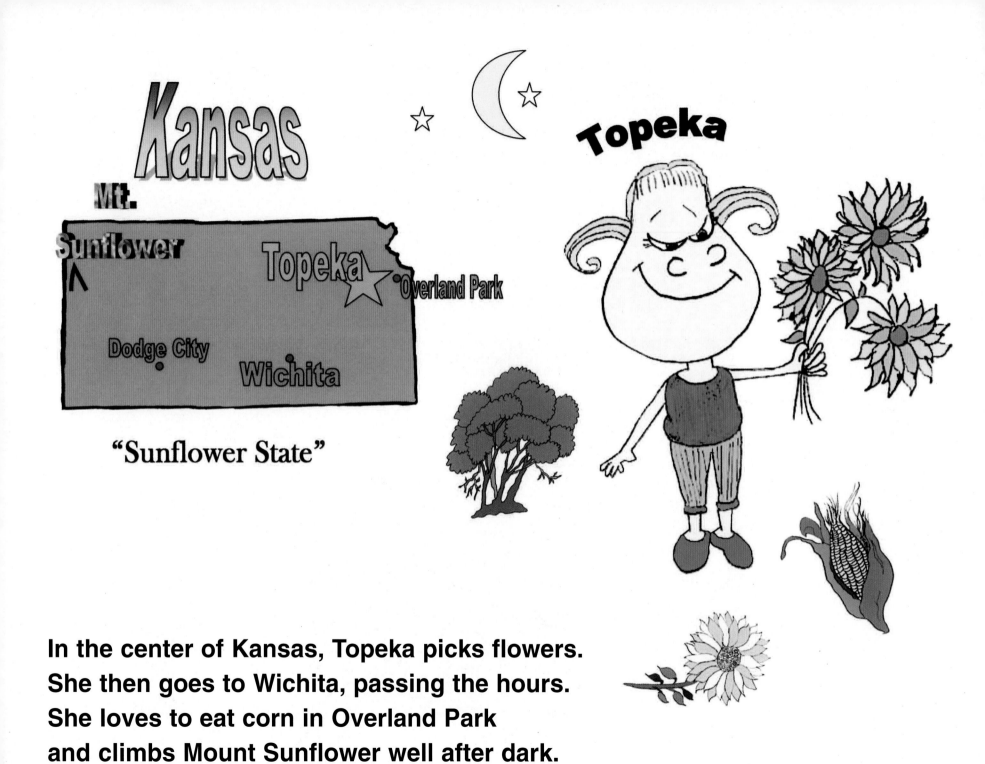

In the center of Kansas, Topeka picks flowers.
She then goes to Wichita, passing the hours.
She loves to eat corn in Overland Park
and climbs Mount Sunflower well after dark.

Kansas

Thirty-fourth State

soybeans

cattle

Bird: Western Meadowlark
Tree: Cottonwood
Flower: Sunflower

wheat

hogs

Seeing the South with Susie

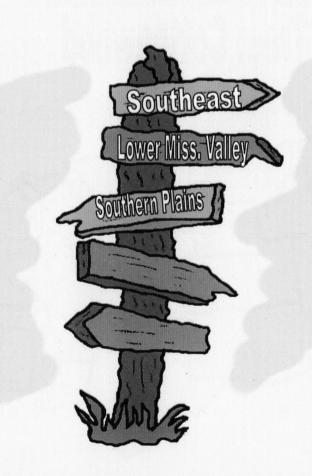

Susie takes a stroll around the Gulf of Mexico.

There are many sights to see, so many friends to know.

She starts off in the Southern Plains and travels toward the coast.

She lays herself upon a beach and happily she roasts.

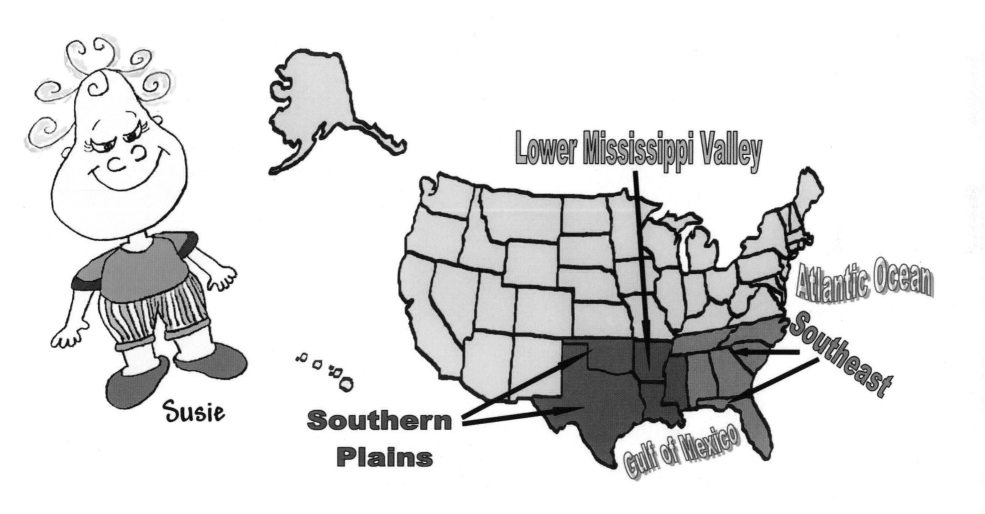

Susie

Southern
Plains

Lower Mississippi Valley

Atlantic Ocean

Southeast

Gulf of Mexico

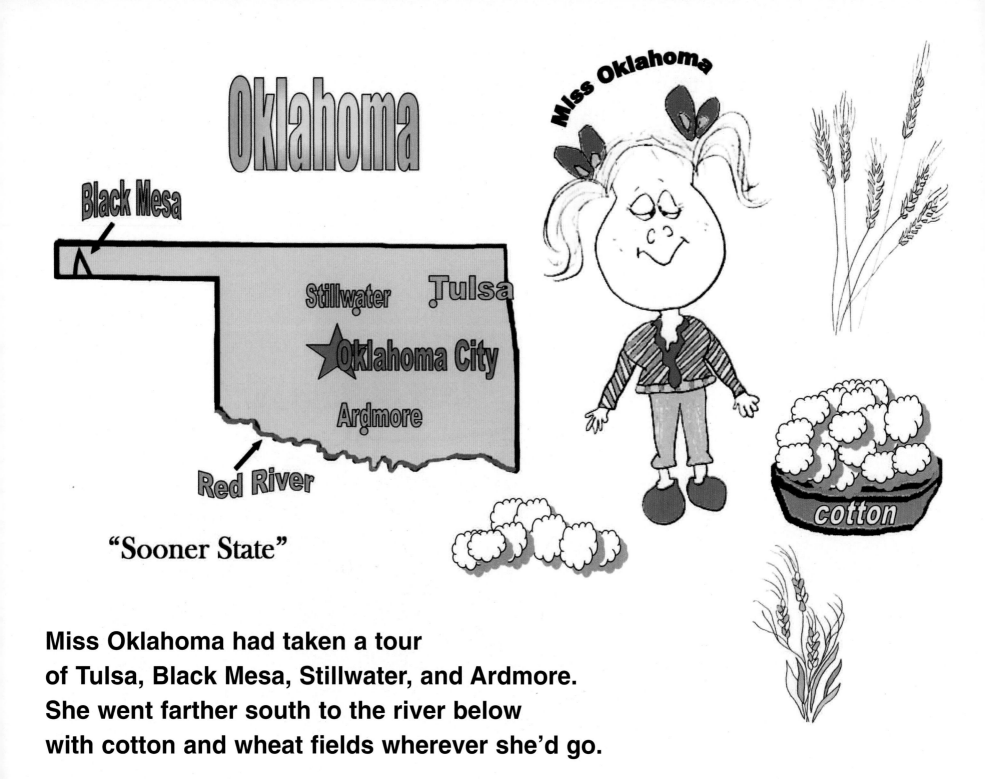

Oklahoma

Black Mesa

Stillwater　Tulsa

★ Oklahoma City

Ardmore

Red River

"Sooner State"

Miss Oklahoma

cotton

Miss Oklahoma had taken a tour
of Tulsa, Black Mesa, Stillwater, and Ardmore.
She went farther south to the river below
with cotton and wheat fields wherever she'd go.

 poultry

Oklahoma

Forty-Sixth State

Bird: Scissor-tailed Flycatcher
Tree: Redbud
Flower: Mistletoe

 cattle/dairy

Austin's a cowboy from the heart of El Paso.
He catches his cattle with a hemp-woven lasso.
There are prairies and lakes, with Houston near the coast.
But the Big Bend Country is what Austin loves most.

 corn

Texas

Twenty-Eighth State

 cotton

poultry

Bird: Mockingbird

Tree: Pecan

Flower: Bluebonnet

 wheat

Beautiful Ms. Baton Rouge lives down in New Orleans.
Every year at Mardi Gras she loves to watch the scenes
Crawfish, rice, and sugar cane are always such a treat.
She sits and dines in restaurants alongside Bourbon Street.

soybeans

Louisiana

Eighteenth State

cotton

Bird: Eastern Brown Pelican
Tree: Bald Cypress
Flower: Magnolia

oil

cattle

eggs and poultry

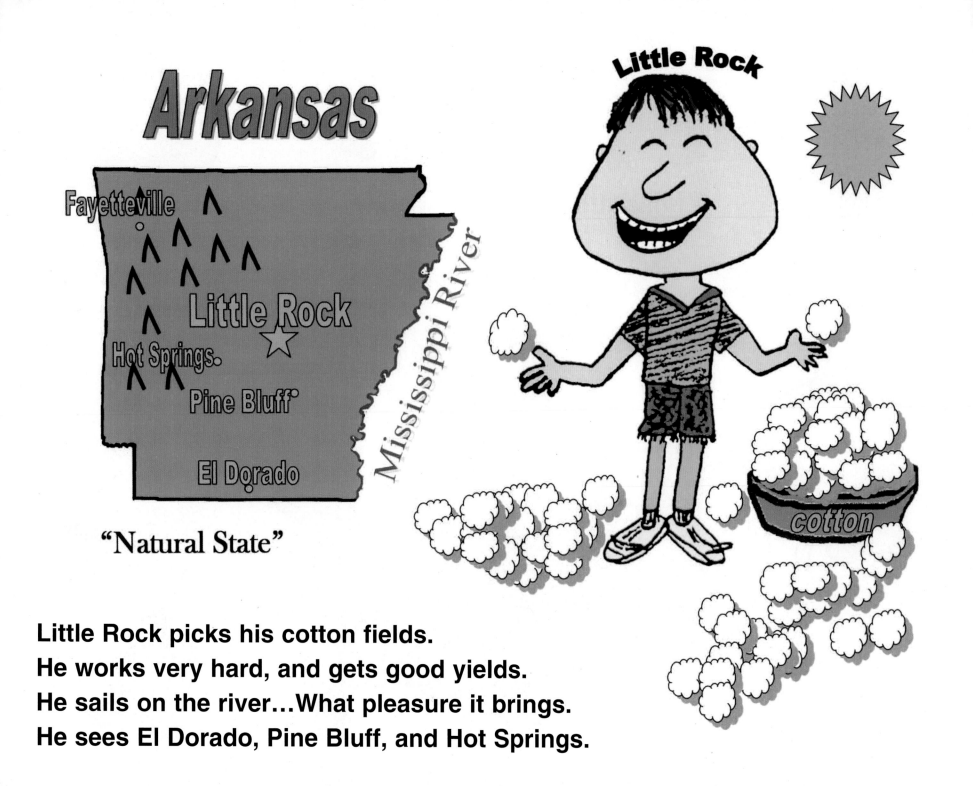

Arkansas

Little Rock

Fayetteville

Little Rock

Hot Springs.

Pine Bluff°

El Dorado

Mississippi River

"Natural State"

cotton

Little Rock picks his cotton fields.
He works very hard, and gets good yields.
He sails on the river…What pleasure it brings.
He sees El Dorado, Pine Bluff, and Hot Springs.

soybeans

Arkansas

Twenty-fifth State

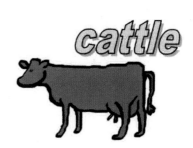

cattle

hogs

Bird: Mockingbird
Tree: Loblolly Pine
Flower: Apple Blossom

rice

eggs and poultry

Mississippi

Mississippi River

Tupelo

Jackson

Gulfport Biloxi

Gulf of Mexico

"Magnolia State"

Jackson

In the great Mississippi, Jackson likes to fish.
Catfish with beans is his all-time favorite dish.
Biloxi and Gulfport are close to the sea,
with countless marinas, great places to be.

Tennessee

Mississippi River

Clarksville

Nashville

Memphis

Cumberland Plateau

Knoxville

Chattanooga

Smoky Mountains

"Volunteer State"

Nashville and Memphis
were both born to sing.
They dream of the fame
that their music will bring.
In the Great Smoky Mountains
and Cumberland Plateau
they book many clubs,
and do show after show.

 cattle

 cotton

Tennessee

Sixteenth State

 hogs

Bird: Mockingbird
Tree: Yellow Poplar
Flower: Iris

 tobacco

soybeans

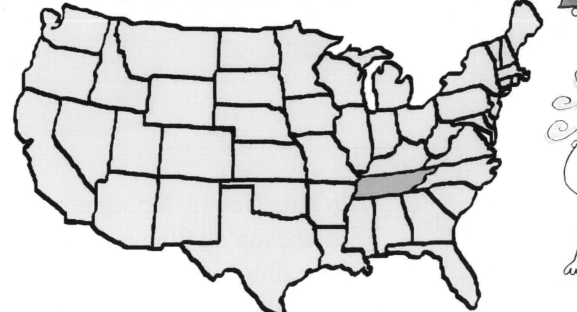

Alabama

Huntsville

Birmingham

Tuscaloosa

Montgomery

Mobile

Gulf of Mexico

Montgomery

SALE

cotton

"Yellow Hammer State"

"The Heart of Dixie"

In Tuscaloosa, Montgomery shops
to escape all that work on the peanut crops.
Alabama cotton makes really fine shirts
and other apparel like blouses and skirts.

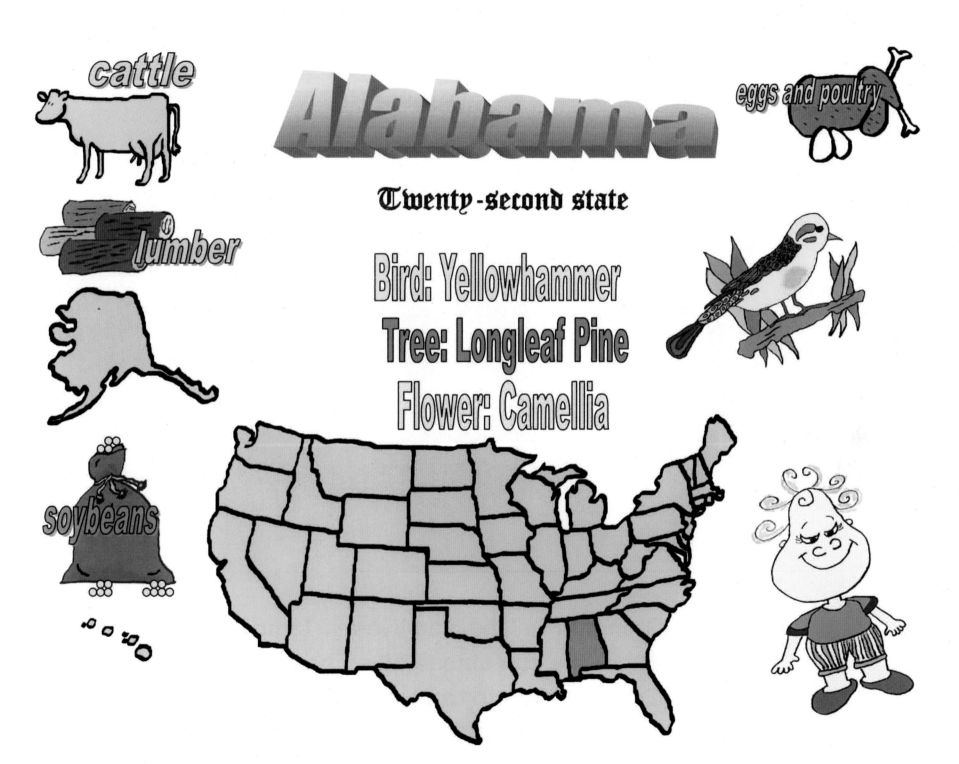

cattle

eggs and poultry

lumber

soybeans

Alabama

Twenty-second state

Bird: Yellowhammer
Tree: Longleaf Pine
Flower: Camellia

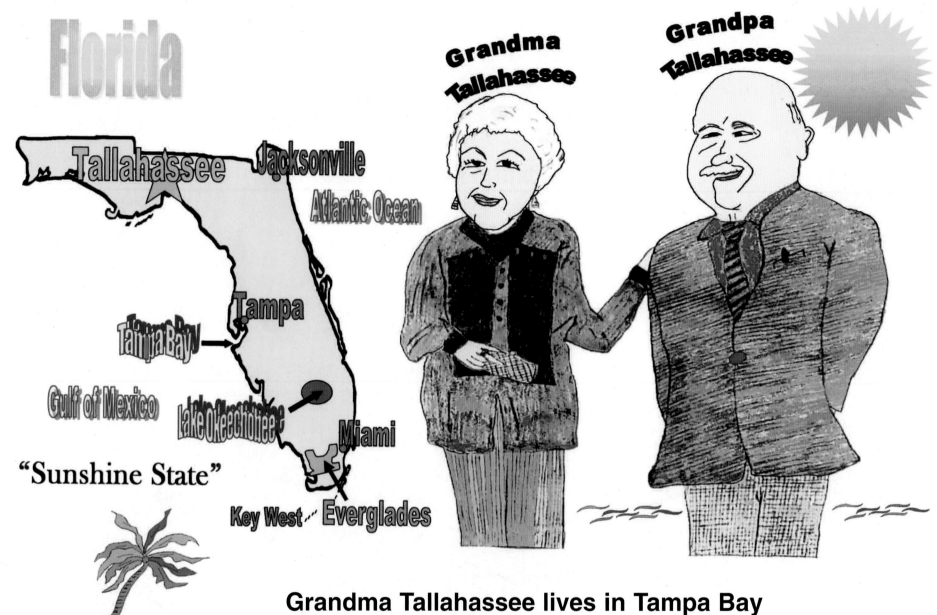

Grandma Tallahassee lives in Tampa Bay
where the sun shines oh so brightly, day after day.
Grandpa likes to travel across the swampy land
past Lake Okeechobee toward the ocean and the sand.

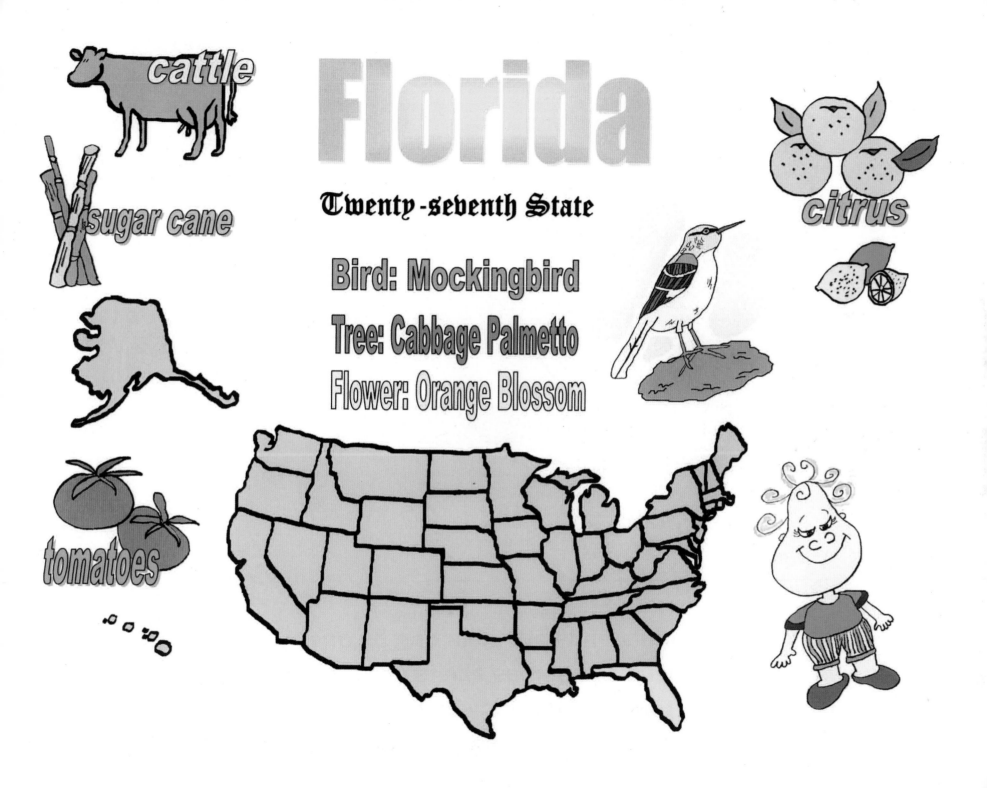

Florida

Twenty-seventh State

Bird: Mockingbird

Tree: Cabbage Palmetto

Flower: Orange Blossom

cattle

sugar cane

tomatoes

citrus

Atlanta grabs some peanuts and eats them one by one.
She throws away the shells as soon as she is done.
She travels to Augusta to buy some juicy peaches,
then heads down toward Savannah to swim on Georgia's beaches.

eggs and poultry

Georgia

cattle/dairy

Fourth State

Bird: Brown Thrasher

Tree: Live Oak

Flower: Cherokee Rose

hogs

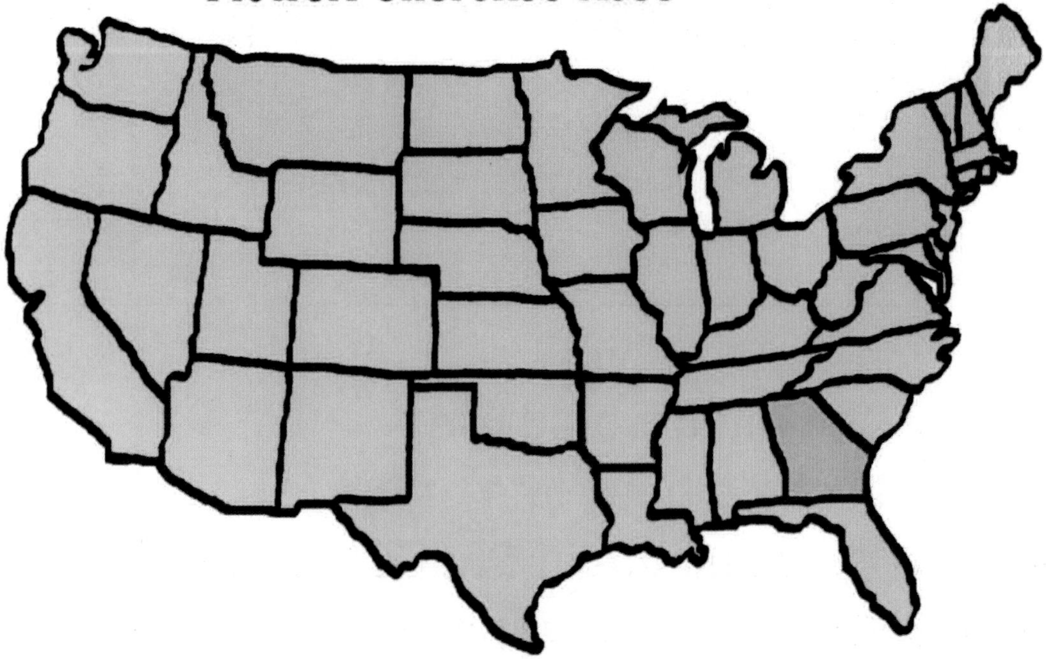

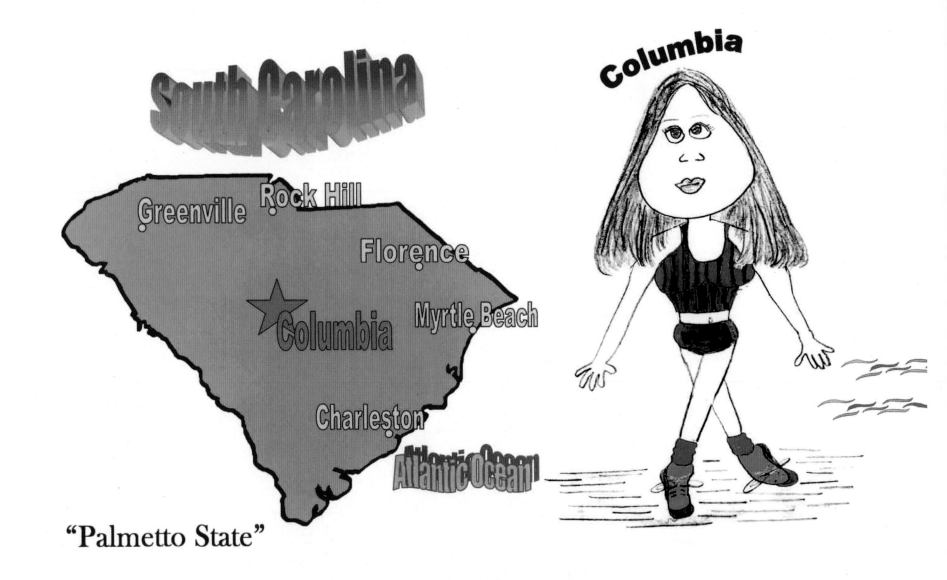

"Palmetto State"

Through South Carolina Columbia would run.
In Greenville and Rock Hill she'd have lots of fun.
She'd dance along some cobblestone in Charleston on the way.
Then she'd go to Myrtle Beach and on the sand she'd lay.

South Carolina

Eighth State

Bird: Great Carolina Wren
Tree: Cabbage Palmetto
Flower: Yellow Jessamine

soybeans

peaches

poultry

hogs

tobacco

cattle/dairy

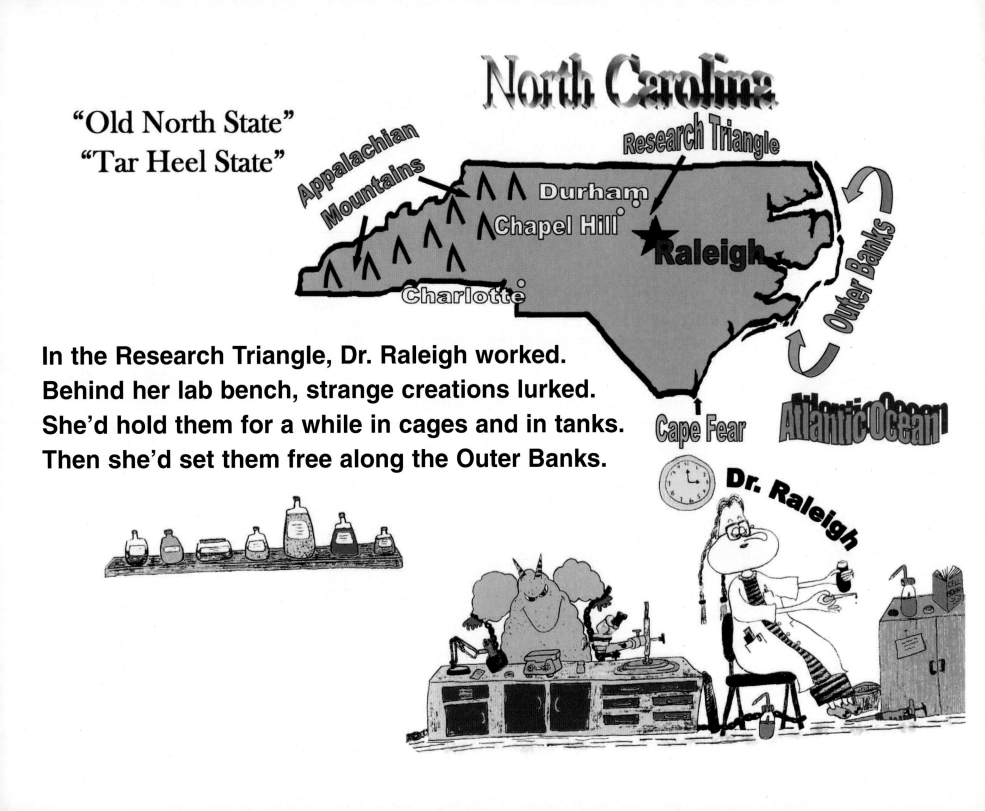

North Carolina

"Old North State"
"Tar Heel State"

In the Research Triangle, Dr. Raleigh worked.
Behind her lab bench, strange creations lurked.
She'd hold them for a while in cages and in tanks.
Then she'd set them free along the Outer Banks.

North Carolina

cattle

tobacco

Twelfth State

Bird: Cardinal
Tree: Longleaf Pine
Flower: Dogwood

soybeans

eggs and poultry

hogs

Exploring the East with Ellie

In the Northeast, Ellie gets on a plane
and flies to see friends in Rhode Island and Maine.
Then the Mid-Atlantic is where she'll pass through
to see friends in New Jersey and Maryland, too.

Ellie

Northeast

Atlantic Ocean

Mid-Atlantic

Augusta dines on lobster, up in Portland, Maine.

Then she's off to Bangor, where she does the same.

The pines of Mount Katahdin rustle in the breeze.

They stay green when the winter comes, and never lose their leaves.

 seafood

Maine

 lumber

Twenty-third State

blueberries

 cattle/dairy

potatoes

Bird: Chickadee

Tree: Eastern White Pine

Flower: White Pine cone and tassel

apples

eggs and poultry

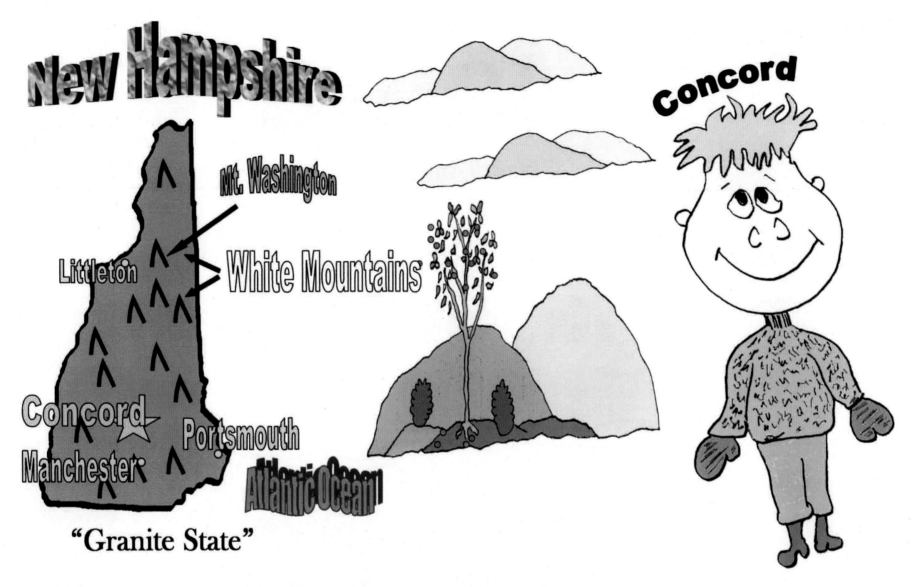

New Hampshire's great White Mountains, young Concord did pass through on his way toward Littleton and old Manchester, too.
Mount Washington was so windy, and chilled him to the bone.
He settled down along the coast, as Portsmouth was his home.

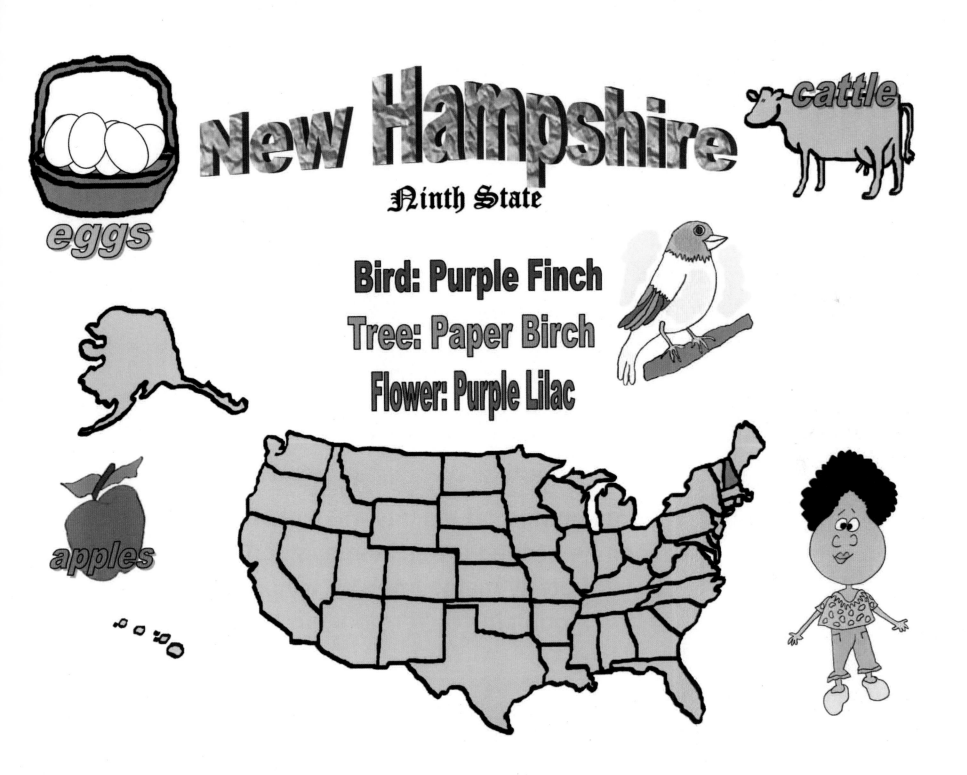

New Hampshire

Ninth State

eggs

cattle

Bird: Purple Finch

Tree: Paper Birch

Flower: Purple Lilac

apples

VERMONT

Montpelier ("Monty")

Lake Champlain

CANADA

Burlington

Montpelier

Green Mountains

Rutland

"Green Mountain State"

Monty started off his day in lovely Lake Champlain.
Then he headed toward the east, on his way to Maine.
Lots of pretty maple trees he would often go past
in the mountains of Vermont, so tall and bold and vast.

Fourteenth State

cattle/dairy

Syrup

maple products

Bird: Hermit Thrush
Tree: Sugar Maple
Flower: Red Clover

apples

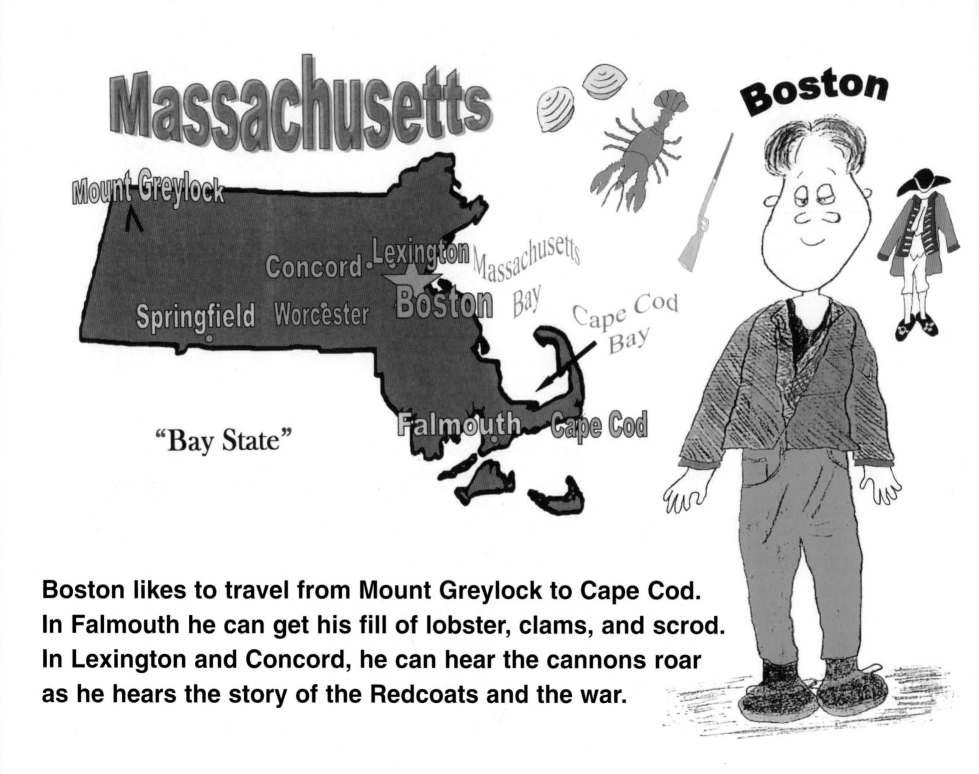

Massachusetts

Mount Greylock

Concord · Lexington   Massachusetts
Springfield   Worcester   Boston   Bay

"Bay State"   Cape Cod Bay

Falmouth   Cape Cod

Boston

Boston likes to travel from Mount Greylock to Cape Cod.
In Falmouth he can get his fill of lobster, clams, and scrod.
In Lexington and Concord, he can hear the cannons roar
as he hears the story of the Redcoats and the war.

Massachusetts

Sixth State

seafood

cranberries

Bird: Chickadee
Tree: American Elm
Flower: Mayflower

dairy
MILK

Rhode Island

Woonsocket
Pawtucket
Providence
Cranston
Newport
Atlantic Ocean

Providence

"Ocean State"

Providence sells jewelry near the mills of Woonsocket.
She does really well and gets cash in her pocket.
Pawtucket and Cranston are where she takes trips,
or to Rhode Island's coast, where her father builds ships.

Rhode Island

Thirteenth State

eggs

MILK

dairy

Bird: Rhode Island Red

Tree: Red Maple

Flower: Violet

On the coast of Connecticut, Ms. Hartford is found
standing just north of the Long Island Sound.
New Haven and Bridgeport are both very near,
and so are the cruise ships at New London Pier.

eggs

Connecticut

Fifth State

cattle

Bird: Robin
Tree: White Oak
Flower: Mountain Laurel

seafood

New York

Albany ("Al")

Lake Champlain

Lake Ontario

Niagara Falls
Buffalo

Lake Erie

Finger Lakes

Albany

"Empire State"

Yonkers/New York City

Long Island

Albany was born and raised in Yonkers.
But the big city traffic was driving him bonkers.
He got in his car and, hardly hitting the brakes,
escaped up north toward fun Finger Lakes.

New York

Eleventh State

cattle/dairy

Bird: Bluebird

Tree: Sugar Maple

Flower: Rose

grapes

apples

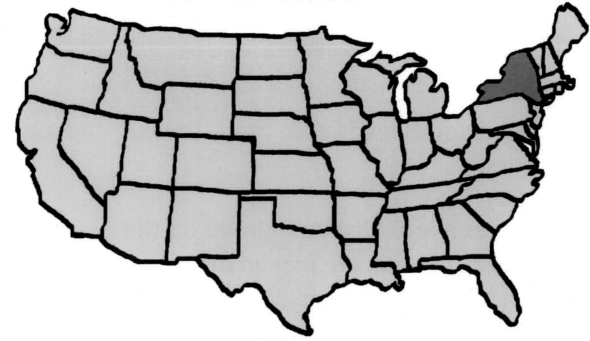

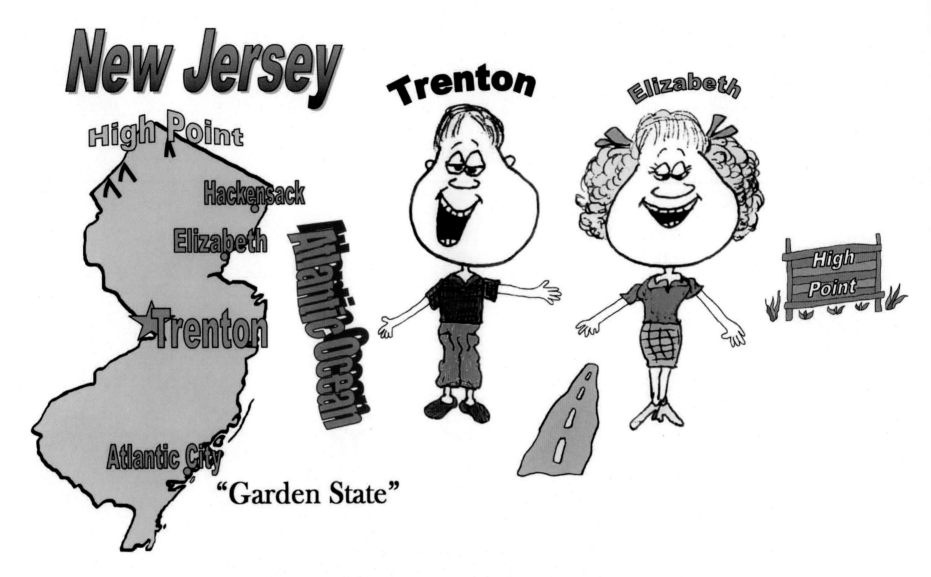

Trenton and Elizabeth drove up the Jersey Pike
to discover all the places they thought that they might like.
Hackensack was really great, as was Atlantic City.
They found the view from High Point to be very, very pretty.

seafood

New Jersey

Third State

horses

Bird: Eastern Goldfinch

Tree: Northern Red Oak

Flower: Violet

dairy

MILK

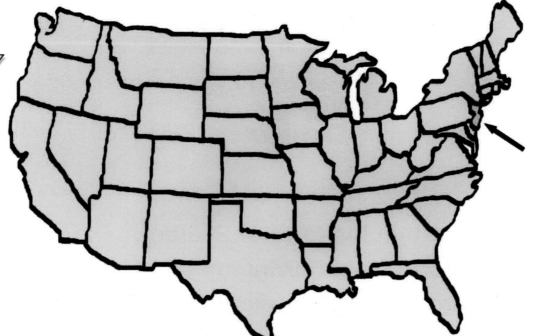

Delaware

"Diamond State"

"Blue Hen State"

"Small Wonder"

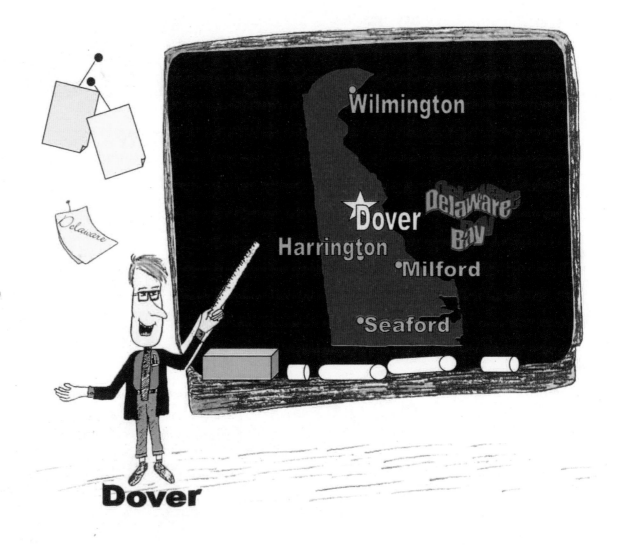

Dover lives in Delaware, within the town of Seaford.
He often travels farther north, past Harrington and Milford.
He walks the coast toward Wilmington, along the Delaware Bay,
selling lots of paper products as he makes his way.

soybeans

Delaware

corn

First State

Bird: Blue Hen Chicken

Tree: American Holly

Flower: Peach Blossom

poultry

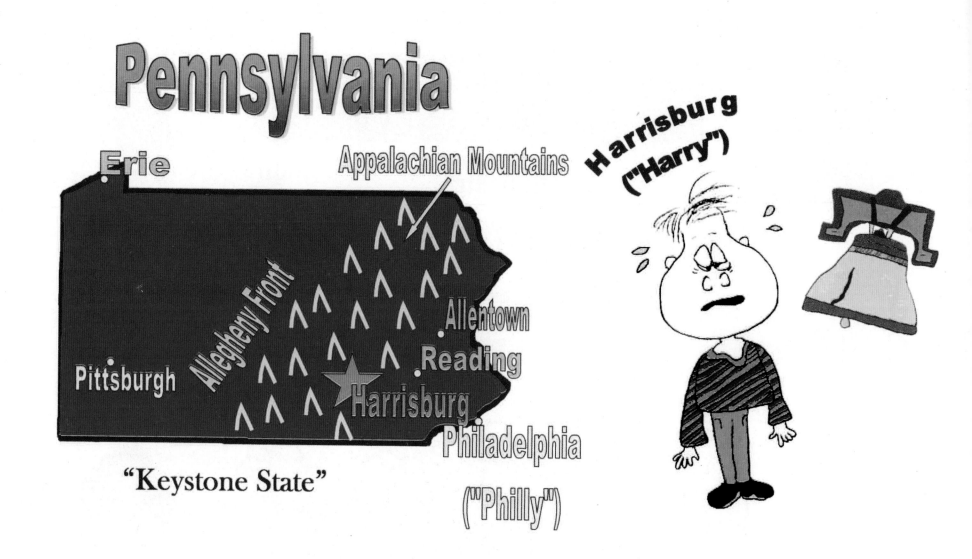

Harrisburg was starting to feel very weary
after hiking through Pittsburgh, Reading, and Erie.
He went toward Allentown from the Allegheny Front,
then reached Philly's Freedom Bell with a groan and a grunt.

poultry

Pennsylvania

cattle

Second State

mushrooms

Bird: Ruffed Grouse

Tree: Eastern Hemlock

Flower: Mountain Laurel

hogs

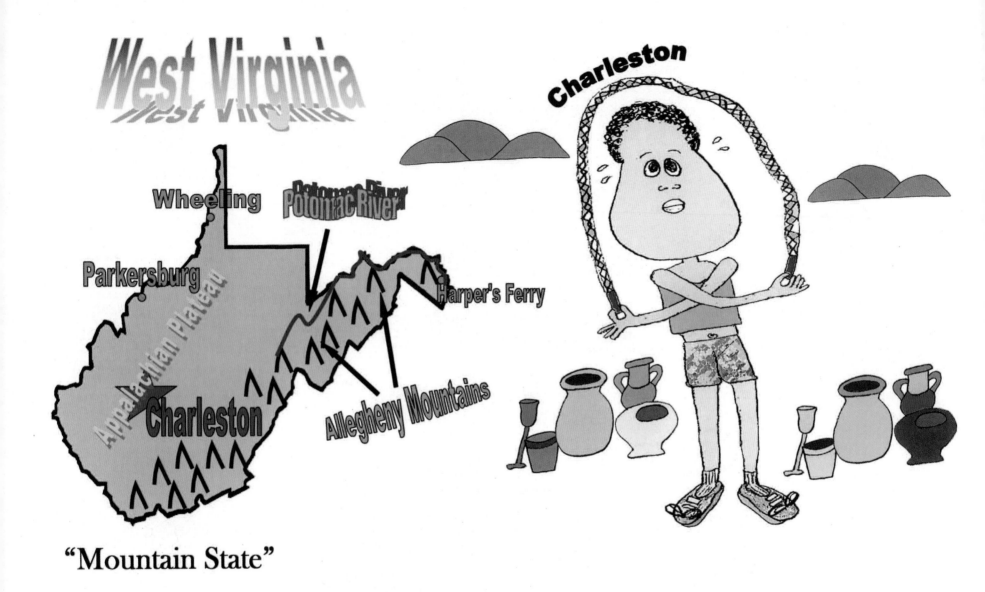

"Mountain State"

Charleston skips across the Appalachian Plateau
and watches the beautiful Potomac River flow.
The mountains and hills he ventures alone,
bearing glass and clay and things made of stone.

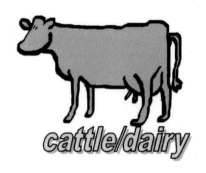

cattle/dairy

West Virginia

Thirty-Fifth State

apples

Bird: Cardinal
Tree: Sugar Maple
Flower: Rhododendron

poultry

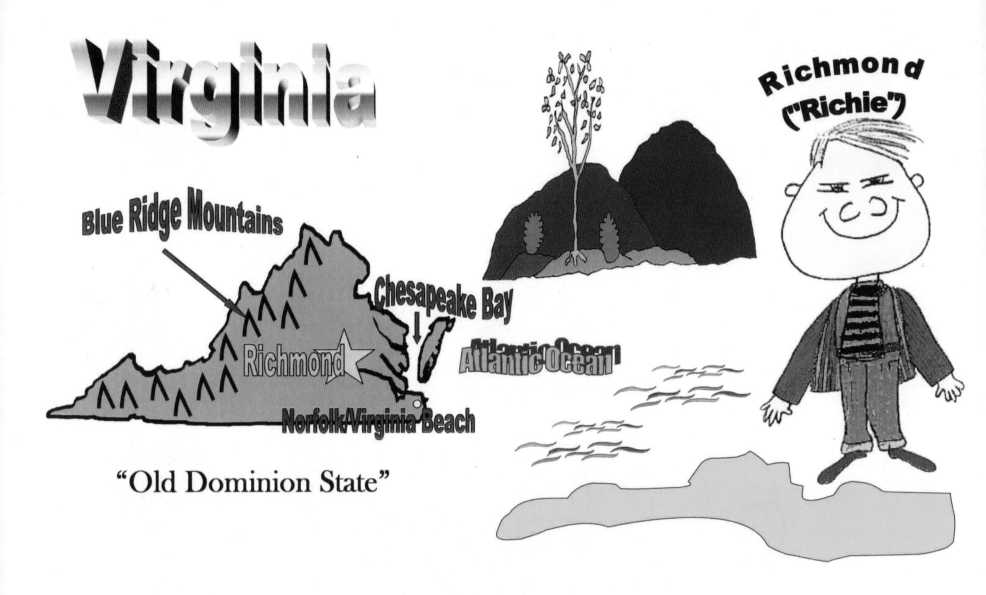

Virginia

Blue Ridge Mountains

Chesapeake Bay

Richmond

Atlantic Ocean

Norfolk/Virginia Beach

"Old Dominion State"

Richmond ("Richie")

Richmond lived for years on Virginia's coastal plain.
The east shore was his home, his pride, and his domain.
But the Blue Ridge Mountains would beckon him away
from Norfolk, Virginia Beach, and Chesapeake Bay.

 soybeans

Virginia

Tenth State

 poultry

cattle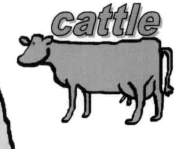

Bird: Cardinal

Tree: Flowering Dogwood

Flower: Dogwood

 tobacco

 hogs

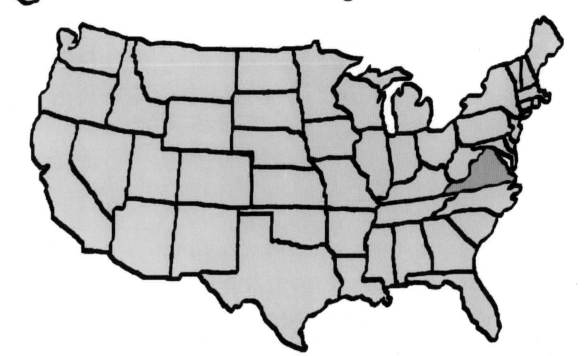

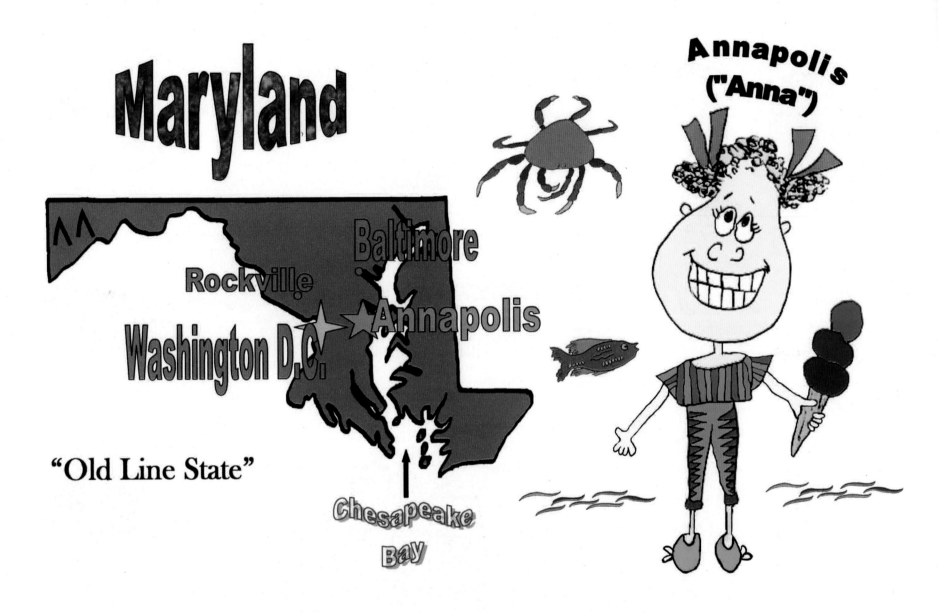

Maryland

Annapolis ("Anna")

Baltimore

Rockville

Washington D.C.

Annapolis

"Old Line State"

Chesapeake Bay

In the state of Maryland, young Anna waits each week
for oh so scrumptious seafood, caught from the Chesapeake.
The crab cakes that her mom makes she really does adore
and she loves to eat the ice cream that's shipped from Baltimore.

Washington, D.C.

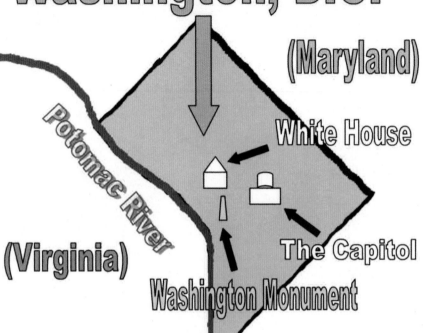

(Maryland)

White House

(Virginia)

Potomac River

The Capitol

Washington Monument

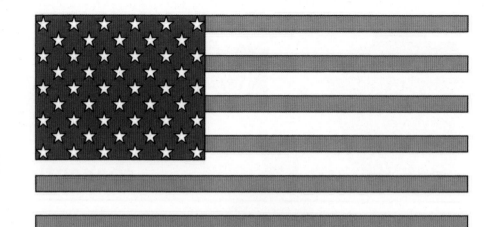

Washington

With no more places to see and roam,
Ellie finally makes her way home.
She meets up with Washington, the best of her mates,
in the capital city of the United States.

To order additional copies of this book,

please send full amount plus $5.00 for

postage and handling for the first book and

$1.00 for each additional book.

Send orders to:

Galde Press, Inc.

PO Box 460

Lakeville, Minnesota 55044-0460

Credit card orders call 1–800–777–3454

Phone (952) 891–5991 • Fax (952) 891–6091

Visit our website at http://www.galdepress.com

Write for our free catalog.

More great children's books included.